GW01086869

CONTENTS

CONTENTS	Page #	CD Track
Introduction	2	1
Foreword	3	
Tuning notes		2
Unit One: The Shapes	4	
Shape 1	4	3
Example 1	6	4
Example 2	6	5
Example 3	6	6
Shape 2	7	7
Example 4	8	
Shape 3	9	8
Example 5	10	
Shape 4	11	9
Example 6	12	
Example 7	12	
Shape 5	13	10
Example 8	14	
Shape 6	14	
Using Chord Tones	15	
Example 9	15	
Unit Two: Blues in C	16	11
Basic Changes	16	
Harmonic Analysis	16	
Subsitutions	17	
Blues In C Solo	18	
Unit Three: Bounce Blues	23	12
Unit Four: Bay Blues	30	13

Transcriptions and additional text by
HARRY HESS

Gibson Herb Ellis Model guitar courtesy of
Paul Jankowski at Gibson Guitars

© 1996 WARNER BROS. PUBLICATIONS
All Rights Reserved

Editors: Colgan Bryan, Aaron Stang
Technical Editor: Glyn Dryhurst
Art Design: Joseph Klucar
Engraving: Andrew Parks

INTRODUCTION

Welcome to *Swing Blues*. This book is part of THE HERB ELLIS JAZZ GUITAR METHOD, a three book series designed to provide you with the skill to "comp" (accompany) and improvise over any standard progression.

The emphasis of this entire series is on fundamental chord progressions common to all jazz standards. Mastery of the material contained in these books will translate into command of any jazz tune, thereby allowing you to expand your repertoire in significantly less time.

Swing Blues' focus is on the 12-bar blues progression which is as rudimentary to jazz improvisation as it is to blues, rock, and country. Like the aforementioned contemporary styles, the roots of jazz are so entrenched in the blues that careful study of one blues tune will rapidly improve your musical knowledge and expand your repertoire into hundreds of songs crossing all stylistic bouderies.

Technical and musical analysis of this pivotal progression is provided in uncomplicated fashion to unlock the door to jazz accompaniment and improvisation.

In addition to *Swing Blues* I would suggest you refer to my books *All the Shapes You Are* and *Rhythm Shapes* to expand on this concept.

FOREWORD

HERB ELLIS is a consummate musician whose stellar career has spanned over sixty years. He's played with all the jazz greats, from the pivotal Oscar Peterson Trio (piano, bass and guitar) to Ella Fitzgerald.

On the included recording, Herb plays just as he does on the gig. Nothing is held back. Everything is explained thoroughly, providing you with the variety of concepts and options that will bring you the most success.

Great care was taken transcribing the examples to provide not only the notation and tablature but the left hand fingerings as well. We've gone the extra mile for players who know how to benefit from Herb's smooth fingering logic which has been carefully refined from well over a half century of playing experience.

Your dedication and patience to this method will be immeasurably rewarded.

UNIT ONE: THE SHAPES

The "Shape System" relates melodic ideas to basic chord shapes instead of relating them to endless scale patterns, modes and arpeggios. This convenient and simple approach saves the player from the drudgery of practicing scales in all positions, including all of the unnecessary, awkward and impractical fingerings. In addition to being an efficient use of practice time, this system allows the player to sound more natural and musical instead of sounding like somebody playing scales.

All five shapes are "movable" which means that they can be played in any key by changing their position on the fret board. The keys and positions that were used in the following diagrams were chosen to relate to some of the musical examples in the book.

SHAPE 1

Shape 1 is shown as a C chord at the fifth fret. The following diagrams are of Shape 1 followed by its corresponding major scale and arpeggio, and its corresponding dominant 7th scale and arpeggio. Your goal is to be able to instantly *visualize* these shapes as references for your lines. This does not mean that you have to play these scales or arpeggios fast to make them work for you.

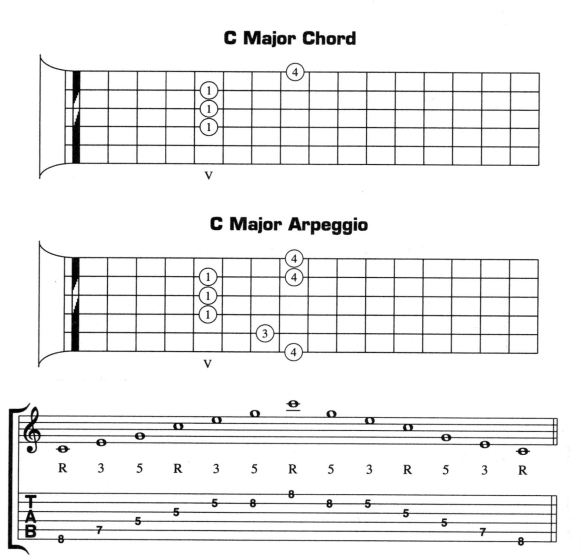

C Major Scale (Ionian Mode)

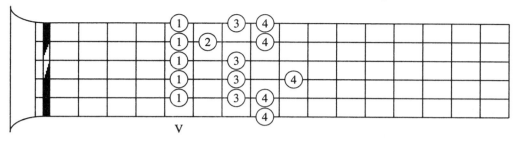

C Dominant 7th Arpeggio

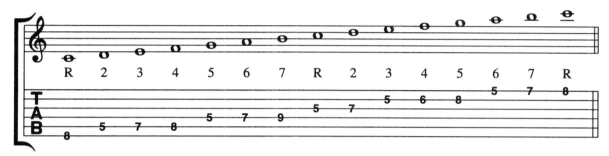

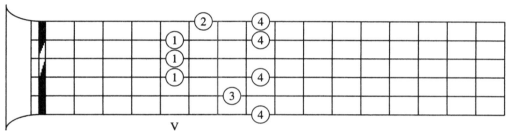

C Dominant 7th Scale (Mixolydian)

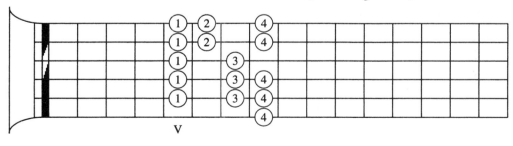

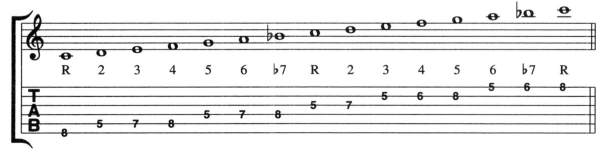

Play the following examples while visualizing shape 1.

Example 1: Cmaj7

Example 2: C7

Example 3: Chromatic

SHAPE 2

Shape 2 is shown as a C chord at the 8th position.

C Major Chord

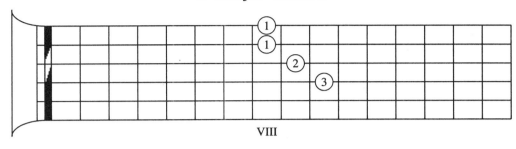

C Major Arpeggio

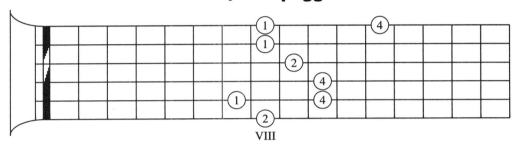

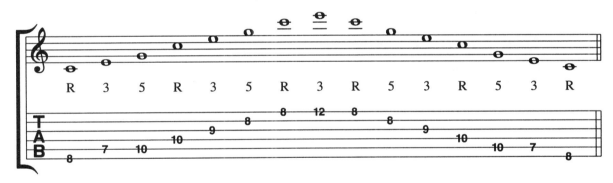

C Major Scale

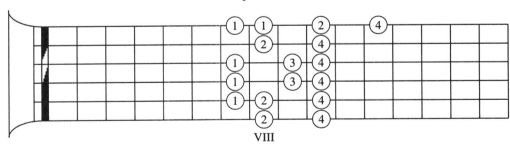

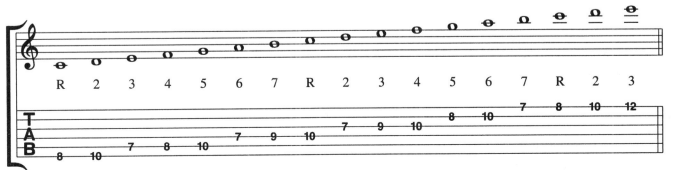

C Dominant 7th Arpeggio

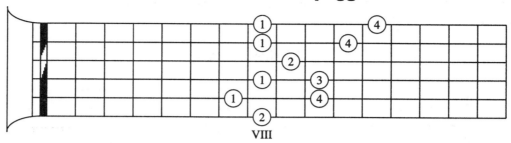

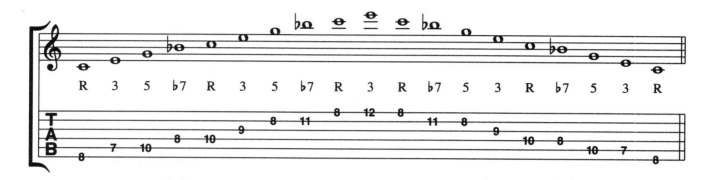

C Dominant 7th Scale

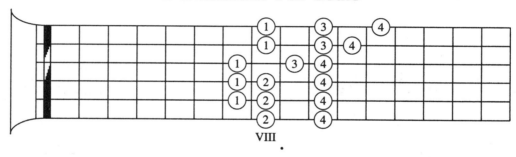

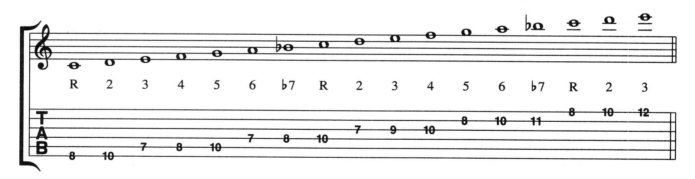

Play the following example while visualizing Shape 2.

Example 4:

SHAPE 3

Shape 3 is shown as a 5th position F chord.

F Major Chord

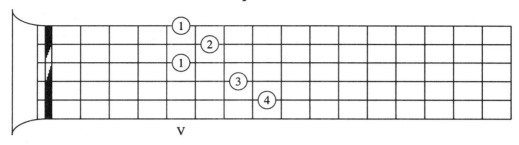

F Major Arpeggio

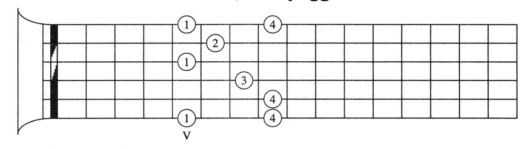

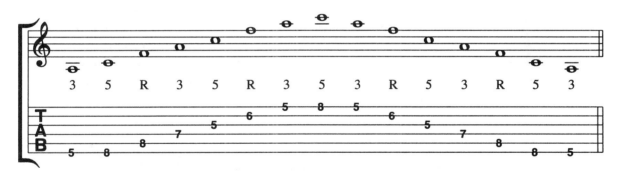

F Major Scale

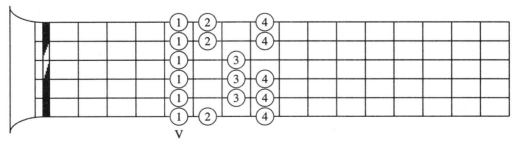

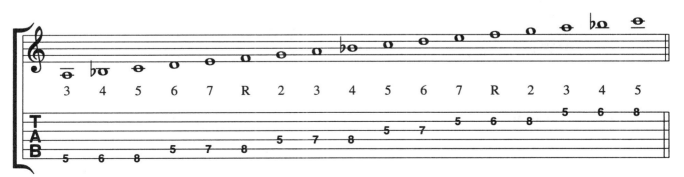

F Dominant 7th Arpeggio

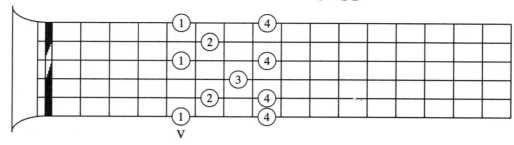

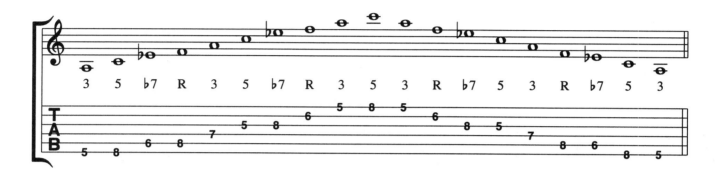

F Dominant 7th Scale

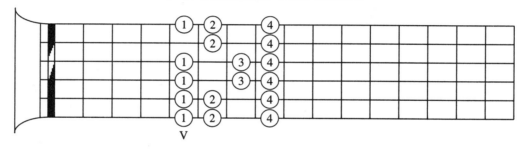

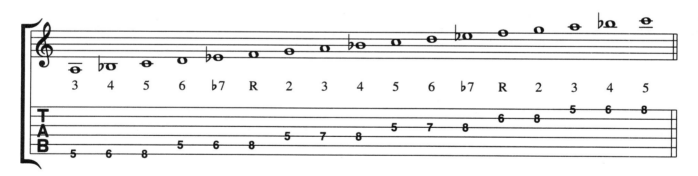

Play the following example while visualizing Shape 3.

Example 5:

SHAPE 4

Shape 4 is shown in 7th position as an F9 chord. Some examples use Shape 4 at the 2nd fret for the C7.

F9 Chord

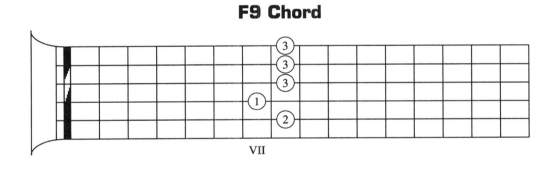

F9 Arpeggio

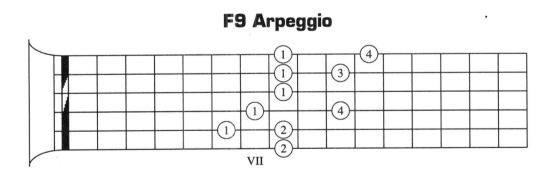

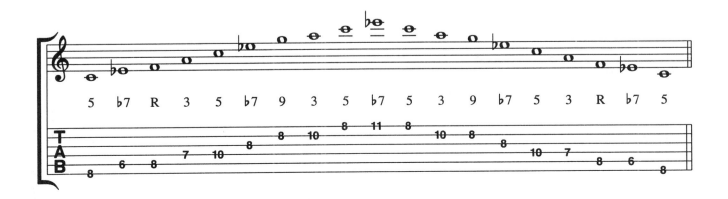

12

F9 Scale

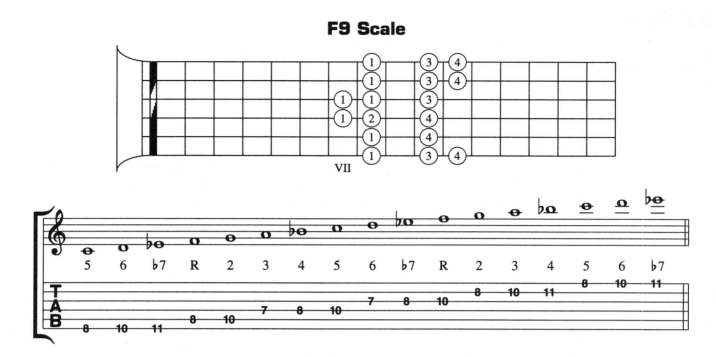

Play the following examples while visualizing Shape 4. Notice the root (F) has been omitted leaving you with an Am7(♭5) arpeggio (A, C, E♭, G) functioning as an F9 chord (F, A, C, E♭, G).

Example 6: F9 Arpeggio

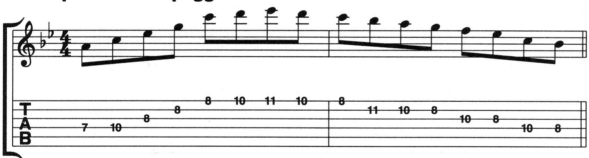

Example 7: F9 "Lick"

SHAPE 5

Shape 5 is shown as a G7 chord in 5th position.

G7 Chord

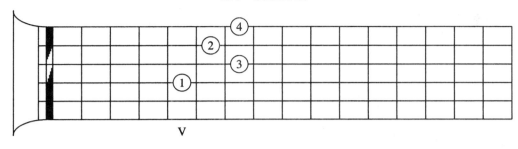

G7 Arpeggio

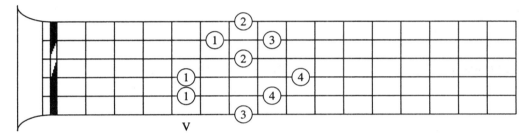

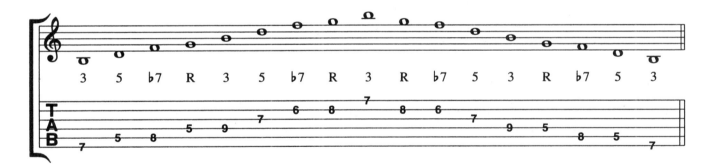

G7 Scale

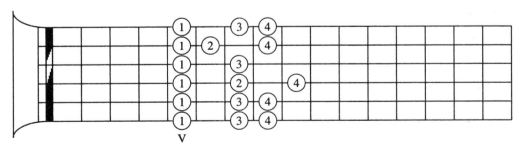

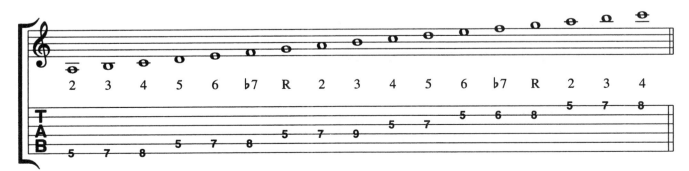

14

Play the following example while visualizing Shape 5.

Example 8:

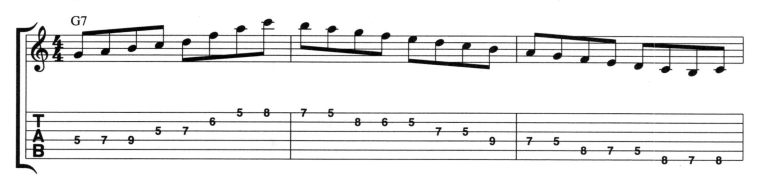

SHAPE 6

There is one more shape that we will call Shape 6 but it is actually a combination of Shape 4 and an inversion of the same dominant 7th chord, fingered two frets higher. Since it is only a variation of a shape that we have already covered, it is not necessary to memorize additional scale shapes to connect with it.

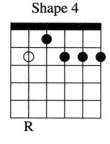

Shape 4

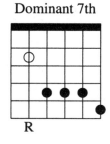

Dominant 7th

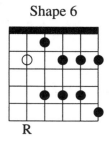

Shape 6

USING CHORD TONES

Rock, Blues and Country guitarists generally have some experience with pentatonic scales or at least have some licks based on these scales. The most common fingering is the following "box" pattern.

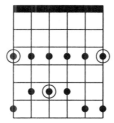

An effective technique for adapting these scales and licks to Jazz is to begin incorporating chord tones. Compare the previous "box" pattern, in the key of G, to the following G7 and C7 arpeggios.

G7

C7

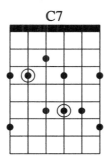

Now play the following example and notice how effectively the additional chord tones connect the melodic lines to the accompaniment.

Example 9:

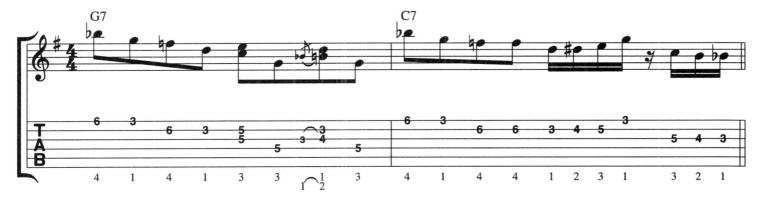

Jazz players often "spell out" the chord changes by using chord tones in their composed or improvised lines. Many players are so skilled at this technique they are able to imply the chord changes without the chord accompaniment. This skill is effective when playing unaccompanied or with a rhythm section consisting of only bass and drums. In addition to the examples in this series, study Charlie Parker lines and solos for more great examples.

UNIT TWO: BLUES IN C

Do not jump ahead to the following chapters until you have thoroughly analyzed this progression and can play it smoothly. Avoid the common mistake that many inexperienced guitarists make of underestimating the value of the accompaniment as an effective source for building solos. Until you have a strong understanding and feel for the chord progression, you will needlessly struggle to come up with strong solos for it.

It is important to point out that accompanying other soloists properly is a valuable skill that will expand your performance and work opportunities. What player doesn't like to be associated with musicians that compliment his or her own playing? If you are a great soloist but lack the ability to comp effectively, you are not going to impress or motivate many players to call you again.

Start comping the examples in this book using a traditional swing feel. You can accomplish this by playing downstrokes, right on the beat, staccato (disconnected) and accenting the second and fourth beat. A common mistake is to chop off the chord too soon. To avoid this, turn your amp volume down and let the chord ring for at least half a beat.

Basic Changes

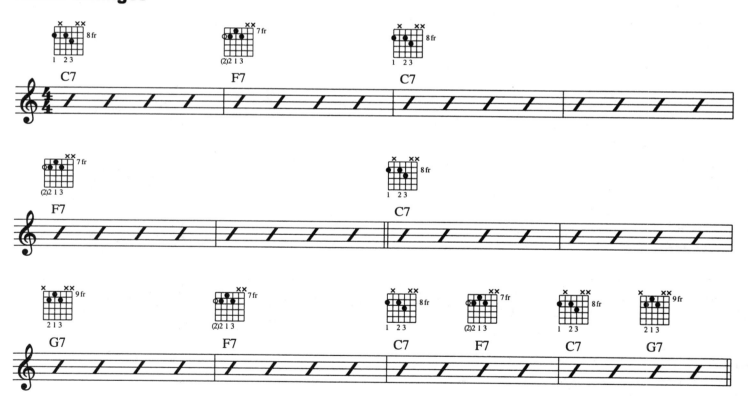

HARMONIC ANALYSIS

Blues in C is a standard 12 bar blues progression. The first four bar phrase primarily revolves around the I chord (C7) with the IV chord (F7) on the 2nd measure to provide some extra movement.

Bars 5 and 6 break away further from the C7 with two measures of the IV chord (F7), and then returning to C7.

Bars 9 and 10 create tension by breaking away from the I chord entirely, starting with one measure of the V chord (G7) for dissonance (tension) followed by one measure of the IV chord.

The last 2 measures are the turnaround which, as the word implies, turns the progression around to the beginning. There are a variety of turnarounds that are commonly used, but this specific example is described as a I - IV - I - V progression.

SUBSTITUTIONS

Substitutions, as the word implies, are chords that are so similar that they can be used to replace each other. Adding substitutes to progressions can add variety and color to an existing progression, and/or help define the movement of the progression more clearly.

Now here is the same progression with some substitutions to give it a little more color: compare these substitute changes to the basic changes.

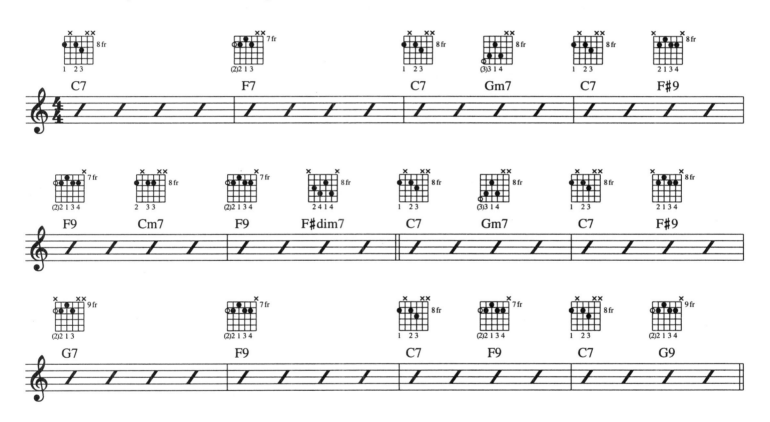

The Gm7 in the third measure is a common substitute for the C7. The Gm7 and C7 are the II - V of the same key: F. Either chord can substitute for the other.

The F#7 chord in the third measure is a "leading chord" to the F7. It is very common to approach a chord from a half step above or below.

The Cm7 chord in the fifth measure is a similar substitute as the third measure. Cm7 and F7 are the II - V chords in the key of B♭.

The F#dim chord in the sixth measure adds some tension and movement to the F7 chord. If you compare the F#dim7 to the F7 you notice that the only difference between the chords is the root.

BLUES IN C SOLO

Before you start this solo or any solo in this book, make an accompaniment tape of yourself playing the progression at slow, medium and fast tempos. This tape will help you apply the soloing examples more efficiently.

When playing these examples, make sure you memorize each solo note for note, taking special care to use the exact fingering indicated under the tablature in each example. Resist from venturing off into your own solos until you have thoroughly learned the examples.

Make sure you visualize the appropriate shapes. This doesn't take more time, but it does take more concentration. Remember, if you don't have a chord reference for your melodic ideas, your ideas may not occur to you at the right time when you are soloing.

The chord diagrams above the staff are only there to remind you of the shapes you need to visualize during those sections of the examples. Do not confuse them with accompaniment. They are only a convenience for you to use until you are able to instantly visualize these shapes yourself.

Notice, for example, the eighth bar of the first chorus, how shape 5 for the G7 chord is indicated one beat prior to the chord change. Anticipating a change is an effective melodic device that is used throughout all of the examples.

BLUES IN C

Example 10:

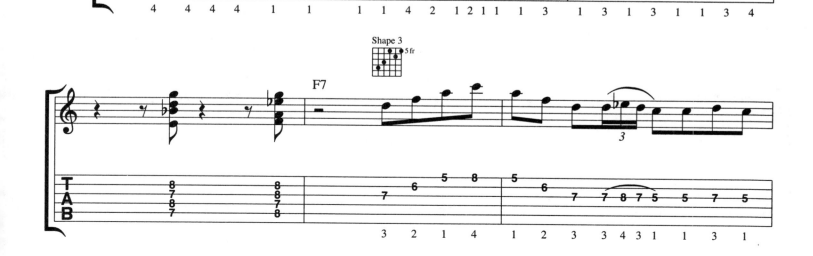

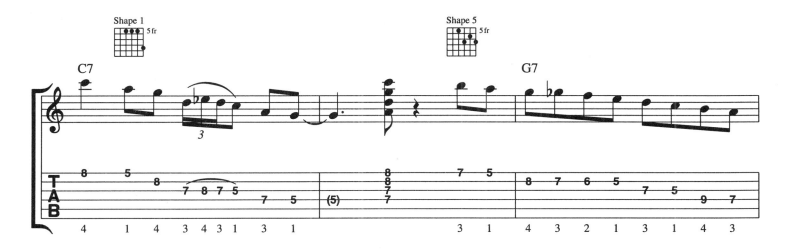

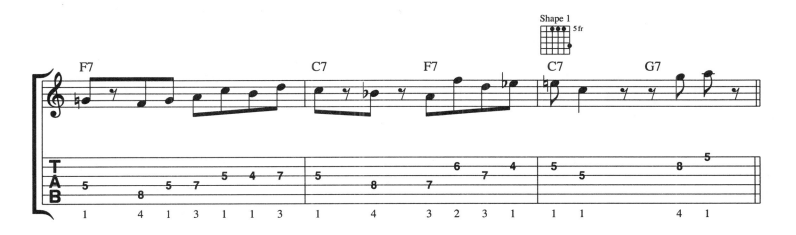

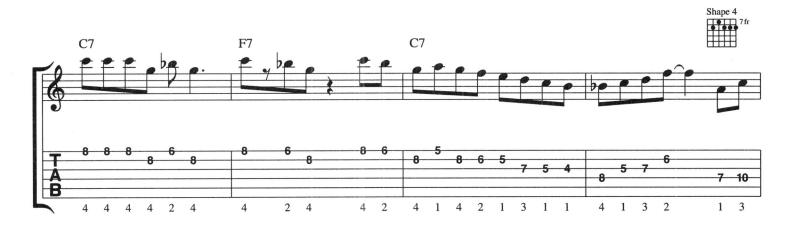

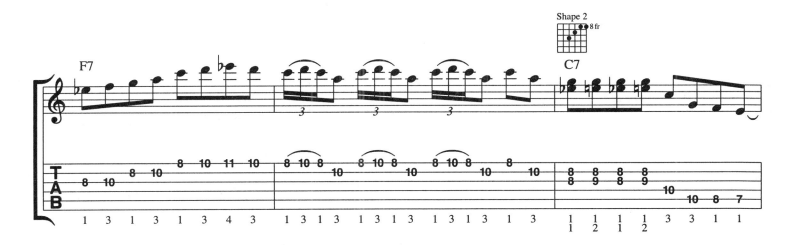

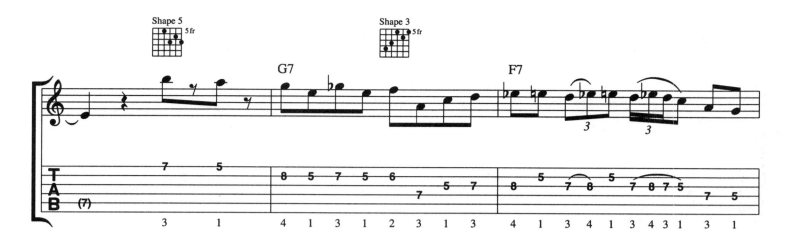

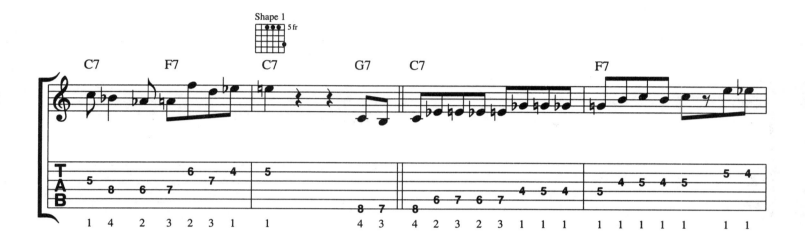

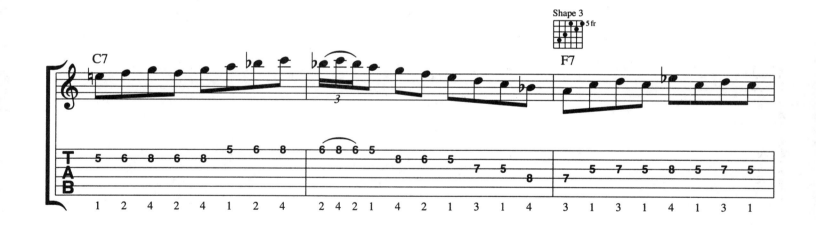

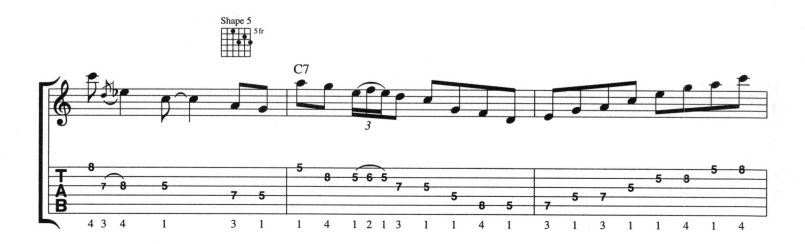

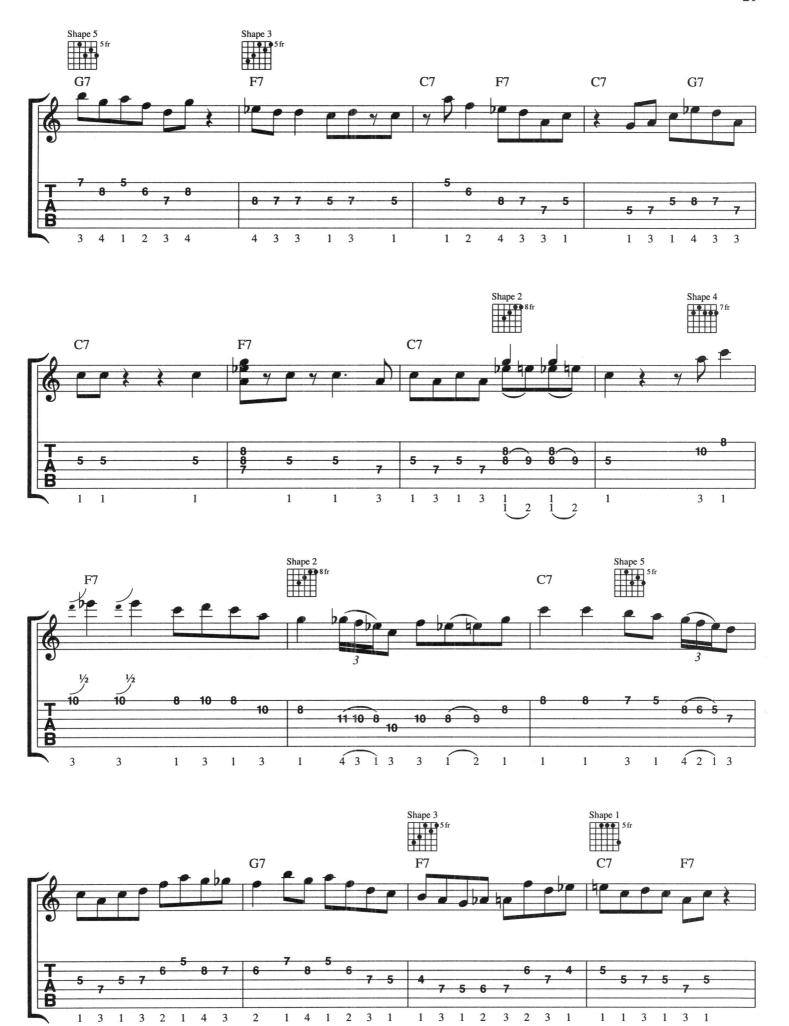

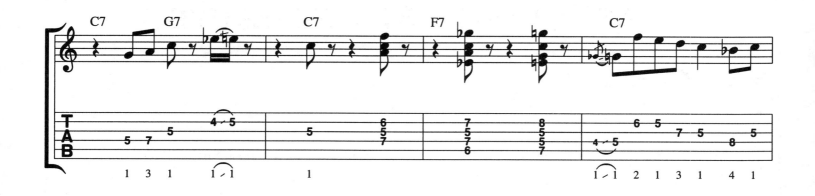

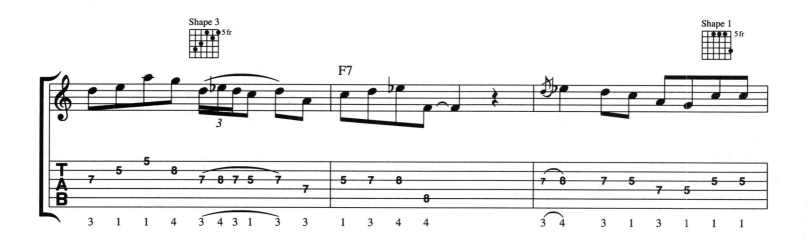

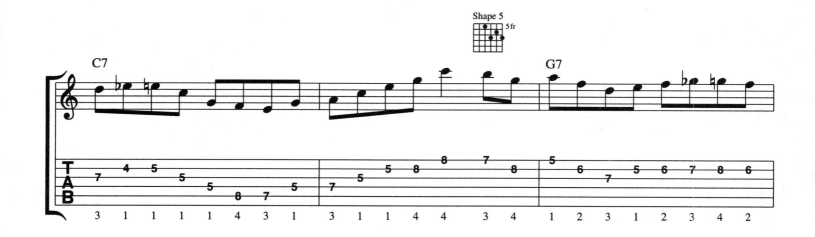

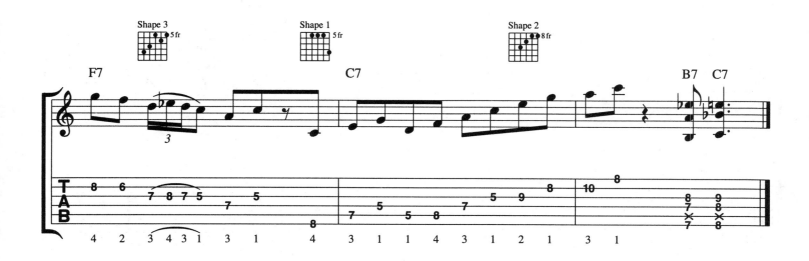

UNIT THREE: BOUNCE BLUES

Bounce Blues is a 12 bar blues in the key of F. The basic changes are about the same as the "Blues in C" progression, but the substitutes and chord voicings give it more variety.

The Bdim chord in the second measure is another example of a dominant chord with the root raised a half step.

The Cm7 and F7, in the fourth bar, are a II - V progression in the key of Bb. Not only does this progression function as a substitute for the F6 chord, but it also leads to the Bb chord in the following measure.

The D7 in the eighth measure is a substitute called a secondary dominant. An inversion for F6 would normally be a Dm7 chord, but it is not unusual to raise the third in the Dm7 chord to make it a dominant chord which leads more effectively to the G7 in the next measure. This substitute works especially well for Blues.

The turnaround is a basic I - V turnaround common to any blues oriented style.

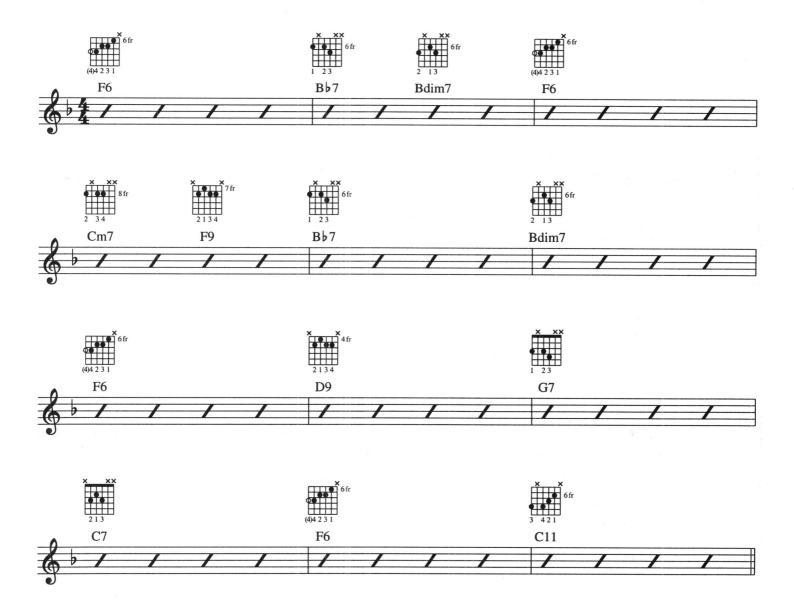

BOUNCE BLUES

Example 11:

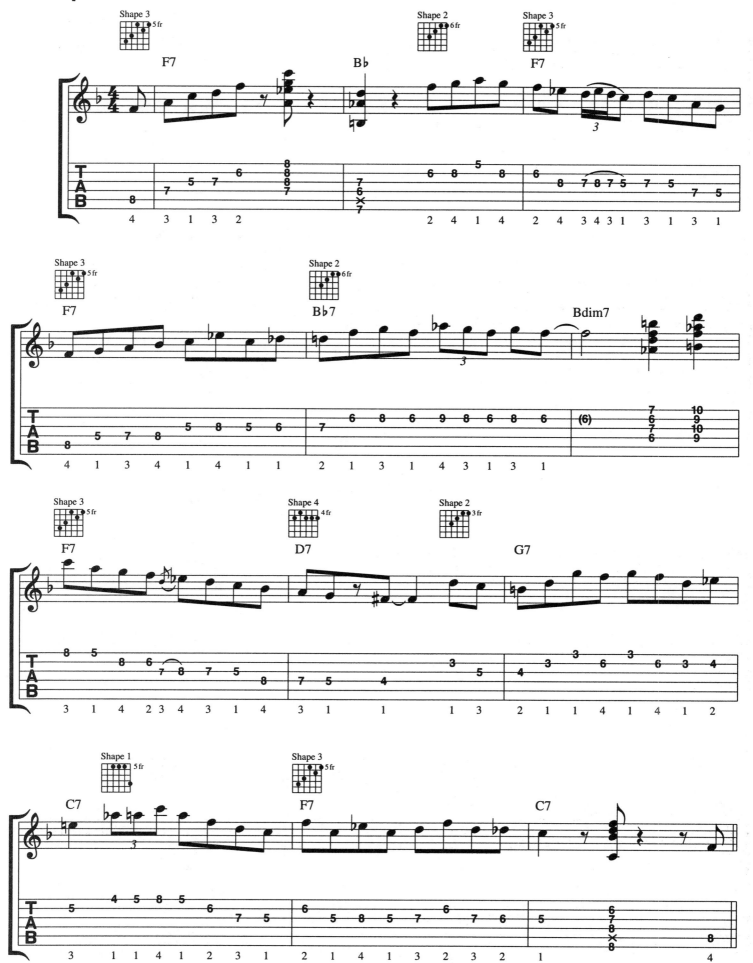

25

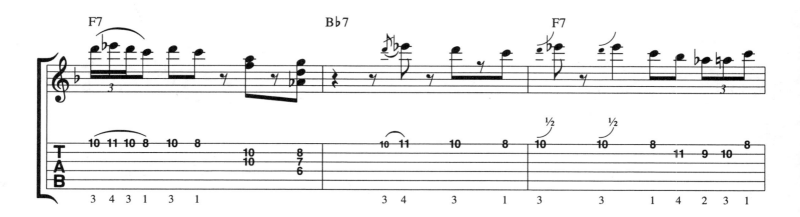

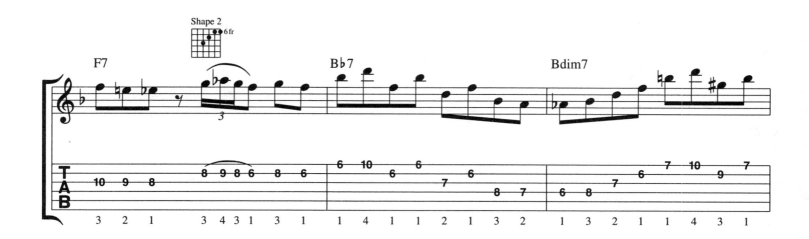

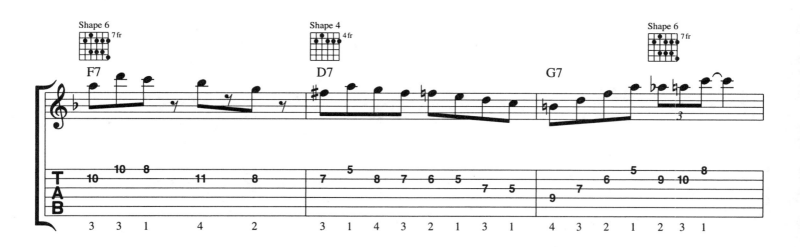

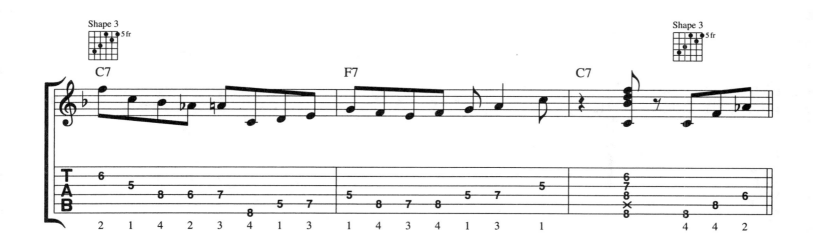

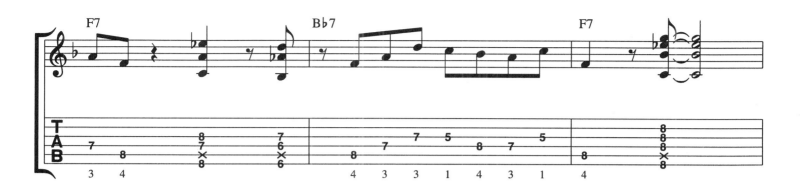

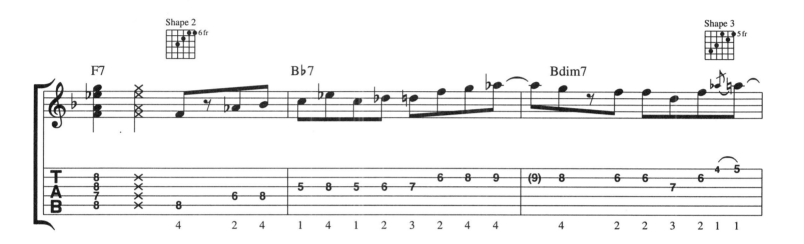

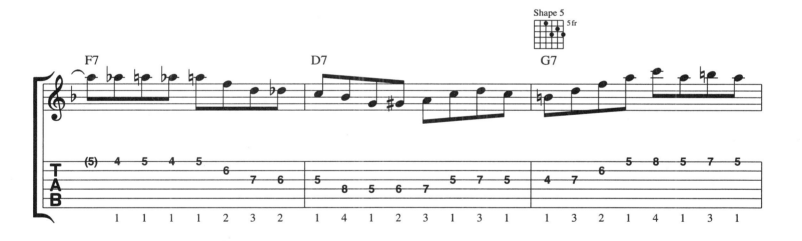

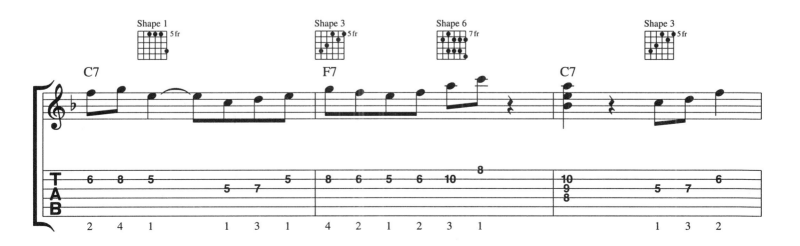

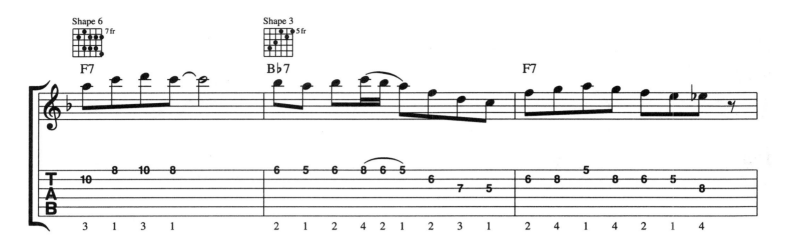

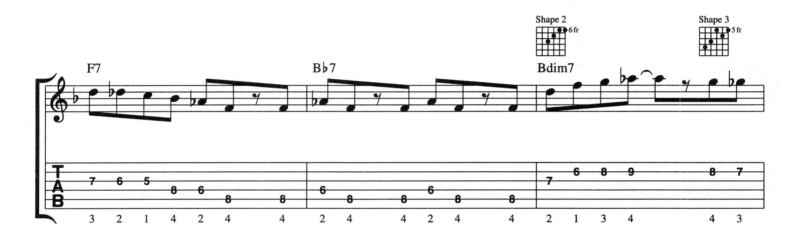

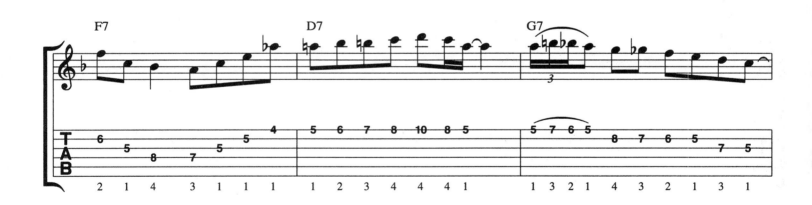

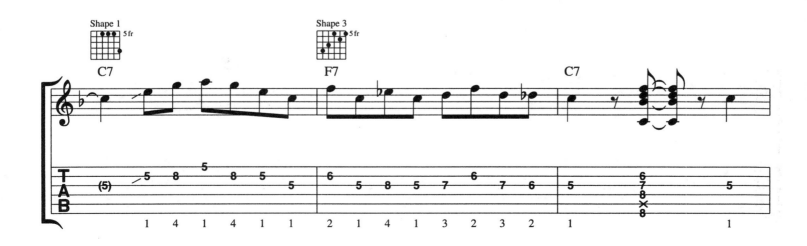

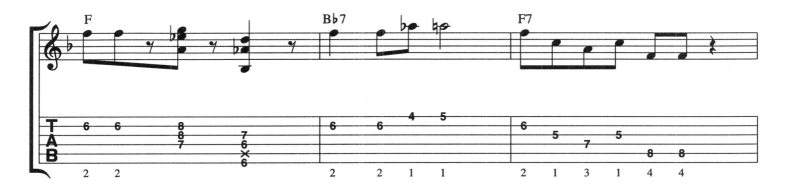

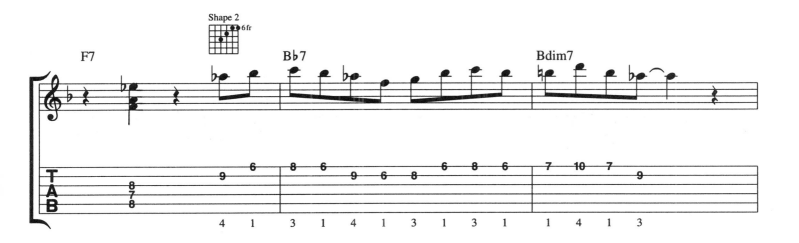

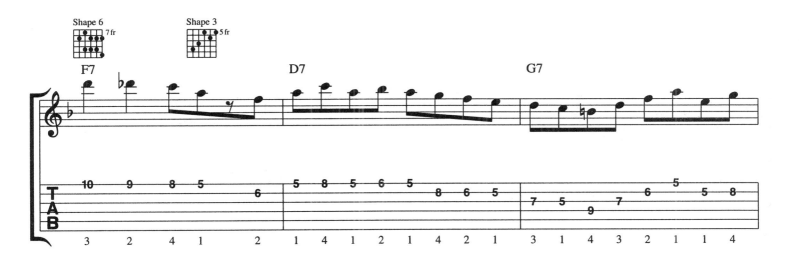

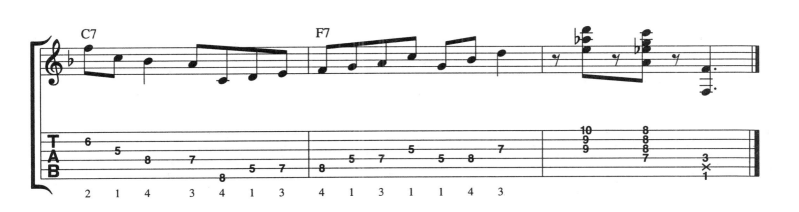

30

UNIT FOUR: BAY BLUES

The first chorus of *Bay Blues* is a 12 bar blues in B♭. The following choruses add various substitues that have been covered in previous examples. The chords in parenthesis are the optional substitutes.

*The C7 works combined with F7.

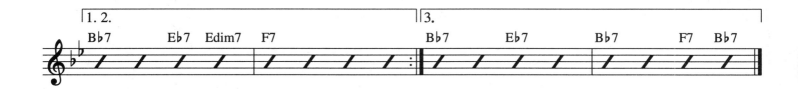

BAY BLUES

Example 12:

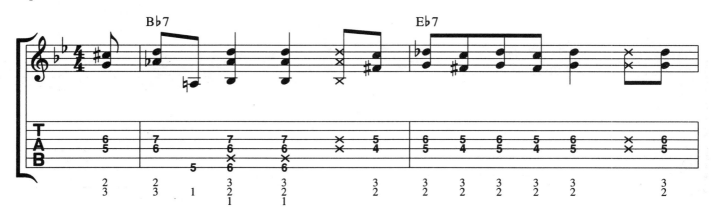

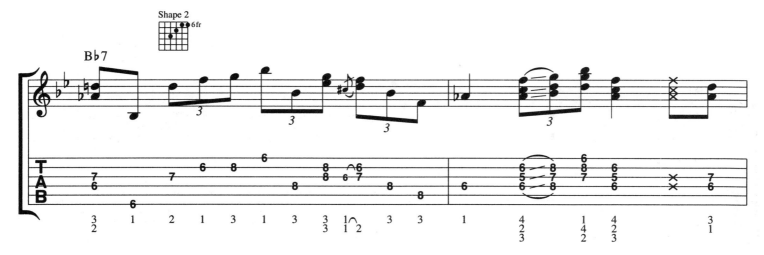

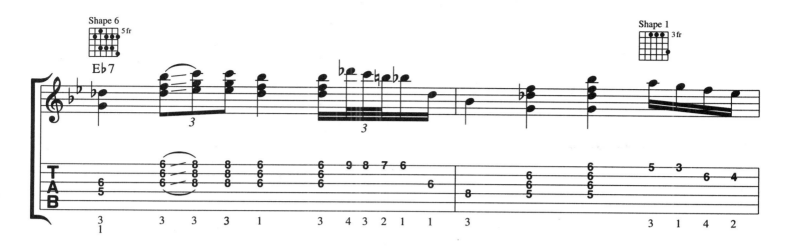

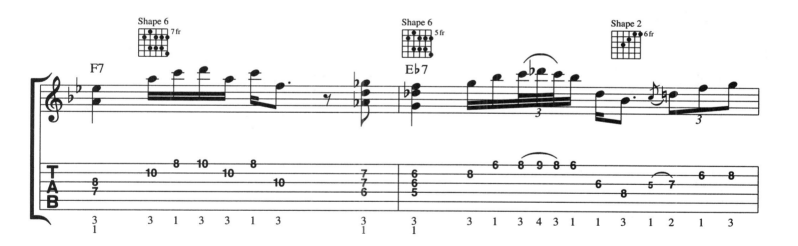

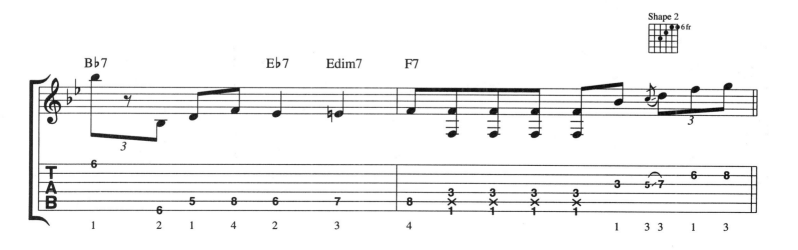

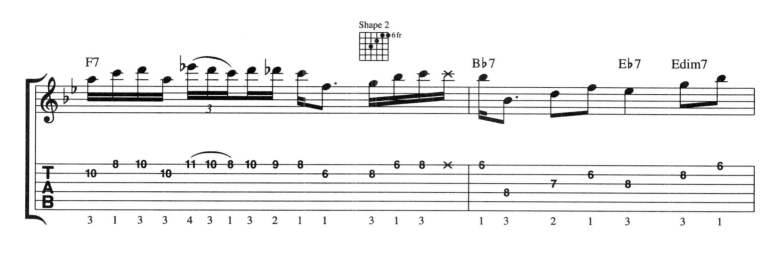

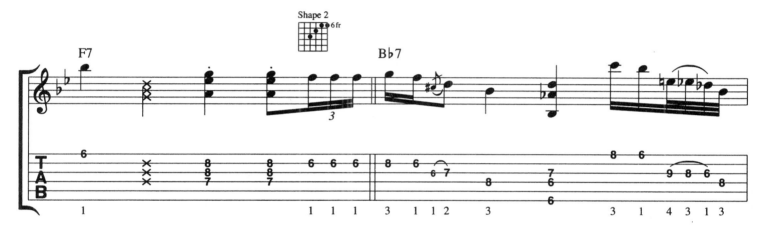

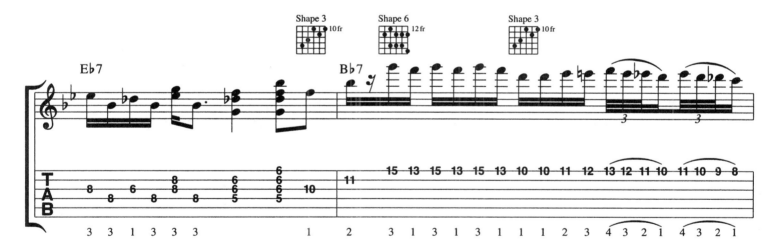

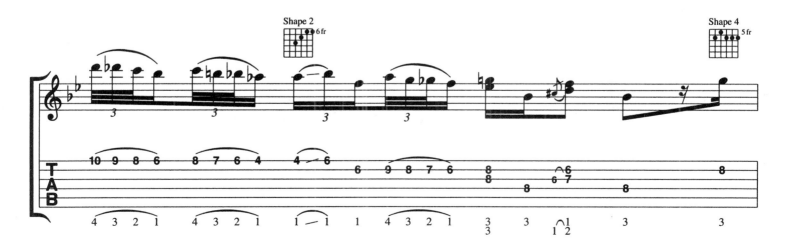

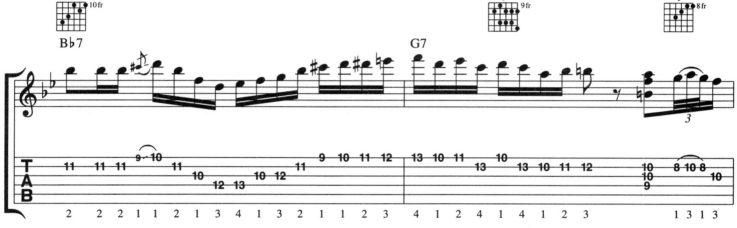

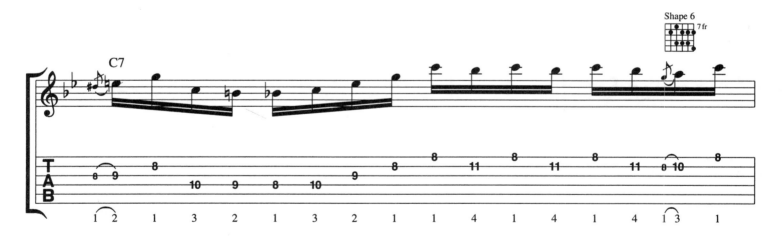

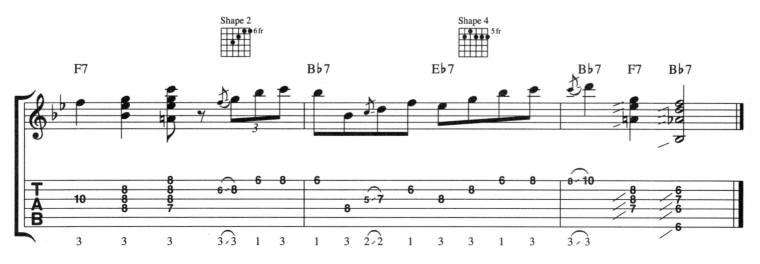

Special thanks to Harry Hess for his contribution to this book.

2 LEGENDARY MASTERS
Herb Ellis and Joe Pass

In the world of jazz guitar, Herb Ellis and Joe Pass have been universally hailed as two of the most important and influential players the music world has ever seen. These incredible videos offer a rare opportunity to get first-hand lessons from two giants of jazz.

HERB ELLIS/
SWING JAZZ SOLOING & COMPING
(REH809)

Herb uses the 12-bar blues progression as a background while he discusses and demonstrates some favorite lines that have made him part of jazz guitar history. He takes you through tuning, chord formations, scales, picking, comping, equipment and melodic ideas, adding new insights with his common sense advice. (60 min.)

JOE PASS/
AN EVENING WITH JOE PASS
(REH843)

An instructional and performance video featuring a concert (with a great trio) plus a pre-concert run-through of jazz classics like "Satin Doll," "All the Things You Are" and more. In clinic, Joe discusses and demonstrates the techniques he employs, chord-melody and "playing what you hear." Booklet included. (90 min.)

JOE PASS/
JAZZ LINES
(REH814)

Joe discusses the scales and arpeggios he uses when improvising. Joe also demonstrates non-stop improvised lines for: major 7th, minor 7th, static and altered dominant 7th chord types plus a special section on turnarounds. Get insight into how Joe "thinks" while improvising. Booklet included. (60 min.)

JOE PASS: BOXED SET
(REH850)

Two Joe Pass videos, *Jazz Lines* and *An Evening with Joe Pass,* packaged together in an attractive slipcover.